T0196930

Living Daily
by the ABCs of
Faith

OGOCHUKWU VERA NANKWE

WESTBOW
PRESS*
A DIVISION OF THOMAS NELSON
& ZONDERVAN

WestBow Press books may be ordered through booksellers or by contacting:

WestBow Press
A Division of Thomas Nelson & Zondervan
1663 Liberty Drive
Bloomington, IN 47403
www.westbowpress.com
1 (866) 928-1240

ISBN: 978-1-5127-5767-5 (sc)

Print information available on the last page.

WestBow Press rev. date: 09/30/2016

Table of Contents

A.

B.

C.

D.

E.

Preface

WHAT IS FAITH?

When I think of faith, I describe it as our acceptance and surrender to the power and reality beyond ourselves. In Hebrews 11:1, faith is defined as "the substance of things hoped for, the evidence of things not seen," and in verse 3, "by faith we understand that the worlds were framed by the word of God, so that the things which are seen were not made of things which are visible."

The Bible says that "we walk by faith, not by sight" (2 Corinthians 5:7). By faith, we believe that God was, is, and will forever be. Through faith, we believe that Jesus is the Son of God and that He came, suffered, and died on the cross to pay the ransom so that we could live.

Faith is very powerful. In many places in the Bible we read the teachings on faith and the positive outcomes. We also read about the men and women of God and their actions, which reflected their faith. Hebrews 11 shows us the children of God and their works of faith: Abel, through his faith in God, offered an exceptional sacrifice that, though it was done many years ago, we still speak of today. Noah, by faith, believed God's command and warning; he built an ark that saved his life and his household's. Abraham obeyed God and went out by faith to a foreign land, not knowing where he was going. He trusted God, who blessed him with the land as his inheritance. Abraham had such a strong faith that even when he was tested to offer his only son for a sacrifice, he did not waver but obeyed. By faith, Moses, disregarding all the trials, led the Israelites out of Egypt and through the Red Sea. By faith, the Israelites encircled the wall of Jericho, sang around it for seven days, and watched the wall fall down. These are just a few of many instances in the Bible where faith was put into action.

In Hebrews 11:6, God says, "Without faith it is impossible to please Him, for he who comes to God must believe that He is, and that He is a rewarder of those who diligently seek Him." Therefore, as children of the Most High God, we ought to live and work by faith, because God's promises are received through faith. This can be seen in the life of Abraham (Romans 4:13–25). When God told him, "I have made you the father of many nations" (Romans 4:17), he never dithered in his faith. Rather, he strongly believed that what God had promised, He would surely bring to pass. Sure enough, Abraham is regarded to this day as the father of many nations. As the descendants of Abraham, those who are true-living beneficiaries of these promises, we have to be strong in our faith and continually put our faith into action, believing the Word of God through daily living by the ABCs of faith.

A: Abide in Christ

"Abide in Me, and I in you. As the branch cannot bear fruit of itself, unless it abides in the vine, neither can you, unless you abide in Me. I am the vine, you are the branches. He who abides in Me, and I in him, bears much fruit; for without Me you can do nothing. If anyone does not abide in Me, he is cast out as a branch and is withered; and they gather them and throw them into the fire, and they are burned. If you abide in Me, and My words abide in you, you will ask what you desire, and it shall be done for you." (John 15:4–7)

By abiding in Christ, you are constantly living your life in Him, connecting with Jesus and having a personal relationship with Him. You are committing your ways into His mighty hands and totally depending on Him. When you abide in Christ, the Savior, you will be saved. Your life will be changed. He will bless you and make you bear much fruit. He will never leave you nor forsake you, as He promised in Hebrews 13:5.

A: Acknowledge Him in All Your Ways

"Trust in the Lord with all your heart, and lean not on your own understanding;In all your ways acknowledge Him, and He shall direct your paths" (Proverbs 3:5–6).

We should acknowledge God in all our ways, because we can easily think we made ourselves who we are. We should bear in mind that everything we have and everything we will ever be is by His grace and mercy, not by our own understanding nor by our own power.

A: ASK TO RECEIVE

"Ask, and it will be given to you" (Matthew 7:7).

"Most assuredly, I say to you, he who believes in Me, the works that I do he will do also; and greater works than these he will do, because I go to My Father. And whatever you ask in My name, that I will do, that the Father may be glorified in the Son. If you ask anything in My name, I will do it" (John 14:12–14).

God always wants us to express our desires to Him; He wants us to come to Him, to ask and to believe.

God did not put any limitations on us when He told us to ask for what we want and believe that whatever we ask in His name we will receive. Therefore, do not limit yourself when you are asking God for anything or doubt in your heart God's ability to provide for you, to heal you, to make a way for you where there seems to be no way, to raise you up, to give you a breakthrough, to break any chain that the enemy has handcuffing you. Do not doubt His ability to set you free from any bondage or deliver you from the hands of your oppressor. Do not doubt His ability to make you triumphant, restore your peace, and give you joy once again. Jesus made this clear to us in John 14:12–14, and He repeated Himself in John 16:23. "Most assuredly, I say to you, whatever you ask the Father in My name He will give you." Now, it is obvious that the decision to ask is in your hands. Why not utilize it? Exercise your faith, put it into action, and watch God move in a mighty way in your life.

B: BELIEVE THE WORD OF GOD

Believing is having faith in God and trusting without waver that He will show Himself mighty in your life.

Believe God's word when He says He knows the thoughts He has for you, as He declared in Jeremiah 29:11–13, thoughts of peace and not of evil, to give you a future and a hope.

Believe His word in Numbers 13:30, which says that you are well able to overcome.

In Deuteronomy 28:1–14, God promised that He will make you the head and not the tail. You shall be above and not beneath. You shall lend and not borrow. He promised that the produce of your body, the produce of your ground, and the offspring of your flocks are blessed. He declared that you are blessed when you come in and when you go out. He promised that He will cause your enemies who rise against you to be defeated before your face. They shall come out against you in one way but will flee before you in seven ways. So now all that is left for you do is to believe in order to make these words come alive.

After the angel Gabriel had appeared to Mary and told her everything that God had sent him to tell her concerning the birth of Jesus Christ, Mary answered, "Behold the maidservant of the Lord! Let it be to me according to your word" (Luke 1:38). Mary believed God's message to her, and her faith helped propel those words to come into existence. This is the kind of faith that a child of God needs to have: an enduring faith that does not doubt for a second God's ability to fulfill promises.

B: BE WATCHFUL

"Be sober, be vigilant; because your adversary the devil walks about like a roaring lion, seeking whom he may devour. Resist him, steadfast in the faith" (1 Peter 5:8–9).

Life is a journey. Throughout this journey you will come across different kinds of people—the good, the bad, and the ugly. Those who cheer you up and help propel you toward your destiny are the good; those who tear you down and fight to block you from reaching your destiny are the bad; those who are wolves in sheep's clothing, who act as if they are laughing with you but in reality are laughing at you, they are the ugly. They will never give you good advice, because they don't want you to succeed. You have to be cautious and vigilant to be able to discern who these people are. You have to be careful not to let anyone mislead you. Stay prayerful and ask God for the spirit of discernment, which will help you recognize the kind of people you are dealing with, those to allow in your inner circle and those to let go of in order for you to become all that God has called you to become.

B: BE WHO GOD HAS CALLED YOU TO BE

Be who God has called you to be, and aspire to be who God has called you to be. Strive always to do His will, and do not yield to the pressure to do what is not right. It may not be easy, especially if you are the kind of person who wants to please everyone around you at the cost of your own pleasures.

One thing you should know is that you can never please everybody, and some people will never be pleased no matter how hard you try. They are the kind that put unrealistic expectations on you. They always take from you. They will drain you of all your resources, emotional and physical, including your time, peace, and joy, if you let them. They believe you are obligated to serve them and will never give back what you invest in them. The only way you can free yourself from this kind of oppression is to be yourself.

Assert yourself and learn to say no to some requests. Saying no may not come easily to you, but you can learn. All you have to do is have faith in God and always desire to do His will, to be who He has called you to be and not who the world wants you to be.

C: CAST YOUR CARE ON HIM

"Cast your burden on the Lord and He shall sustain you; He shall never permit the righteous to be moved" (Psalm 55:22). "Casting all your care upon Him, for He cares for you" (1 Peter 5:7).

Casting your care on the Lord means committing every burden, worry, and problem into His mighty hands, knowing that whatever is going on in your life, God will take care of it. He will see you through. God knows the end from the beginning, and He wants us to know that He is still the Alpha and the Omega, as He declared in Revelation 1:8. He is still El Shaddai, the Almighty (Genesis 17:1). In every circumstance, during trials and tribulations, be still and know that God is God, as He declared in Psalm 46:10–11. Even when you walk through the valley of the shadow of death, remember that God is with you (Psalm 23:4).

In Matthew 11:28–30, Jesus said, "Come to Me, all you who labor and are heavy laden, and I will give you rest. Take My yoke upon you and learn from Me, for I am gentle and lowly in heart, and you will find rest for your souls. For My yoke is easy and My burden is light." If your burden feels unbearable, remember Jesus, your true and faithful friend who laid down His life for us (John 15:13). Also, remember the following song, written by Joseph M. Scriven in 1855, to cheer you up and remind you of what you need to do in times of difficulty.

What a friend we have in Jesus,
All our sins and griefs to bear!
What a privilege to carry
Everything to God in prayer!
Oh, what peace we often forfeit,
Oh, what needless pain we bear,
All because we do not carry
Everything to God in prayer!

Have we trials and temptations?
Is there trouble anywhere?
We should never be discouraged—
Take it to the Lord in prayer.
Can we find a friend so faithful,
Who will all our sorrows share?
Jesus knows our every weakness;
Take it to the Lord in prayer.

Are we weak and heavy-laden,
Cumbered with a load of care?
Precious Savior, still our refuge—
Take it to the Lord in prayer.
Do thy friends despise, forsake thee?
Take it to the Lord in prayer!
In His arms He'll take and shield thee,
Thou wilt find a solace there.

Blessed Savior, Thou hast promised
Thou wilt all our burdens bear;
May we ever, Lord, be bringing
All to Thee in earnest prayer.
Soon in glory bright, unclouded,
There will be no need for prayer—
Rapture, praise, and endless worship
Will be our sweet portion there.

C: COMMIT YOUR WAY TO THE LORD

"Commit your way to the Lord, trust also in Him, and He shall bring it to pass. He shall bring forth your righteousness as the light, and your justice as the noonday" (Psalm 37:5–6).

Committing your way to the Lord may sound simple and self-explanatory, but often we think we can do without God. That is a big mistake, because without God, we can do nothing. So we should commit our way, everything we do, to the Lord at all times. The Word of God says that when we commit our way to the Lord, He will direct our paths (Proverbs 3:6; 16:3).

D: DELIGHT IN THE LORD

"Delight yourself also in the Lord, and He shall give you the desires of your heart" (Psalm 37:4).

To delight yourself in the Lord is to find pleasure, satisfaction, and peace of mind in everything that is of God or pertains to God. When you delight yourself in the Lord, your heart will yearn for God. You will always desire to dwell in His presence, because in His presence there is fullness of joy (Psalm 16:11). In His presence, there is anointing that breaks every yoke of failure, addiction, backwardness, sickness, sadness, and oppression. Delight yourself in the Lord to enjoy unlimited access to His presence and the benefits that go along with it.

D: DRAW NEAR TO GOD

"Draw near to God and He will draw near to you" (James 4:8).

You draw near to God through prayer and reading and meditating on the Word of God daily. When you do all these, God said He will draw near to you, and of course when God is nearer to you, you are in good hands because God promises He will never leave you nor forsake you (Hebrews 13:5). So, may your daily prayers and songs be for God to draw you nearer to Him (Hebrews 10:22, Zechariah 1:3, Psalm 1).

E: EXPERIENCE HIS PRESENCE, HIS POWER, AND HIS GRACE

You experience God's presence, power, and grace by engaging yourself in prayer. With God's presence comes a special kind of peace and joy that the world can never give. In His presence, there is fullness of joy and anointing that breaks every yoke of failure and oppression. So may your desire be a continual dwelling in the house of the Lord (Psalm 23:6; Psalm 27:4).

With God's presence comes His grace that never ceases and His mercies that never come to an end. They are new every morning, and great is His faithfulness (Lamentations 3:22–24).

It is also crucial that when you go before the presence of God, you acknowledge Him with thanksgiving and a shout of joy, (Psalm 95:2–3), because His faithfulness is great. We live morning to morning by His mercy, and all we have His hand has provided. Our God is always faithful, and Ephesians 3:20 tells us that He is able to do exceedingly and abundantly beyond all we could ever ask or think.

F: FEAR NOT

"'Fear not, for I am with you; be not dismayed, for I am your God. I will strengthen you, yes, I will help you, I will uphold you with My righteous right hand.'

"Behold, all those who were incensed against you shall be ashamed and disgraced; they shall be as nothing, and those who strive with you shall perish. You shall seek them and not find them—those who contended with you. Those who war against you shall be as nothing, as a nonexistent thing. For I, the Lord your God, will hold your right hand, saying to you, 'Fear not, I will help you.'" (Isaiah 41:10–13)

"Do not be afraid of sudden terror, nor of trouble from the wicked when it comes; for the Lord will be your confidence, and will keep your foot from being caught." (Proverbs 3:25–26)

"Be strong and of good courage, do not fear nor be afraid of them; for the Lord your God, He is the One who goes with you. He will not leave you nor forsake you." (Deuteronomy 31:6)

I believe just like Franklin D. Roosevelt 1933, that "The only thing we have to fear is…fear itself", but know that God "has not put the spirit of fear in you, but of power and of love and of a sound mind" (2 Timothy 1:7). Have faith that God is with you every step of the way. Do not allow yourself to be consumed by fear. Remember that the Lord is your light and your salvation; He is the strength of your life (Psalm 27:1).

Do not let the fear of failure keep you from trying out new things or attempting to change in any way. Step out in faith. Make the move; be the change you want to see, and watch God do amazing things in your life, for He is with you and will always be with you.

Even when someone tries to tarnish your image or falsely accuse you, fear not. Have faith in God and believe that He will surely be your vindicator.

F: FORGIVE AS YOU HAVE BEEN FORGIVEN

> "Therefore, as the elect of God, holy and beloved, put on tender mercies, kindness, humility, meekness, longsuffering; bearing with one another, and forgiving one another, if anyone has a complaint against another; even as Christ forgave you, so you also must do. But above all these things put on love, which is the bond of perfection." (Colossians 3:12–14)

> "For if you forgive men their trespasses, your heavenly Father will also forgive you. But if you do not forgive men their trespasses, neither will your Father forgive your trespasses." (Matthew 6:14–15)

Remember this important fact: we are not worthy. No one is. This is why the Word of God says all have sinned and fallen short of God's glory (Romans 3:23). God's hand is not too short to save nor His ear deaf to our prayers, but our sin keeps us away from Him (Isaiah 59:1–2). Psalm 130:3 tells us that if God kept a record of our sins, no one would escape His condemnation. But we serve a faithful and merciful God, who said in 2 Chronicles 7:14, "If My people who are called by My name will humble themselves, and pray and seek My face, and turn from their wicked ways, then I will hear from heaven, and will forgive their sin and heal their land."

So let us always go before the throne of grace and mercy to ask God to cleanse us of our trespasses. Let us ask Him not to cast us away from His presence or to take His Holy Spirit from us. Let us ask God to restore in us the joy of His salvation and "to renew a steadfast spirit" within us (Psalm 51:10). I believe that if we pray this prayer with all our heart, God will surely answer us, for He says in Psalm 51:17 that a broken spirit and a contrite heart He will not despise.

On the other hand, forgiveness between people is not only about the person who did something wrong to you: it is also about you and God. When you forgive, it keeps you right with God and makes your life better. It keeps your heart free from feelings of resentment.

Be aware of the modern days Pharisees, those you can never please no matter how hard you try. If they existed during the time of Jesus, they still exist in this day and age. After all Jesus did for them, they wanted Him crucified. Disregarding of all the humiliation and betrayal, Jesus said, "Father, forgive them, for they do not know what they do" (Luke 23:34). So if anyone has hurt you and you really don't know what to say or do, just say, "God, forgive them, for they do not know what they are doing."

In Matthew 18:21–22, Peter asked Jesus, "Lord, how often shall my brother sin against me, and I forgive him? Up to seven times?" Jesus answered, "I do not say to you, up to seven times, but up to seventy times seven." This means you have to keep on forgiving in order to move on with your life and not spend a moment of your precious time in anger, bitterness, or sadness.

But does this mean you have forgotten what happened to you? Perhaps not. You may need to remember what happened in order to avoid similar humiliation or pain in the future.

G: GIVE CHEERFULLY AND GENEROUSLY

"But this I say: He who sows sparingly will also reap sparingly, and he who sows bountifully will also reap bountifully. So let each one give as he purposes in his heart, not grudgingly or of necessity; for God loves a cheerful giver. And God is able to make all grace abound toward you, that you, always having all sufficiency in all things, may have an abundance for every good work" (2 Corinthians 9:6–8).

We should always give generously, for there is more blessing in giving than in receiving. In Proverbs 3:9–10, the Word of God says, "Honor the Lord with your possessions, and with the firstfruits of all your increase; so your barns will be filled with plenty, and your vats will overflow with new wine."

G: GIVE THANKS TO THE LORD

"Give thanks to the Lord, for He is good! For His mercy endures forever" (1 Chronicles 16:34; Psalm 107:1; 136:1).

As the children of the Most High God, we ought to always give thanks and praise to almighty God for His goodness, grace, and mercy over our lives. We should always thank God regardless of our circumstances, because He knows the end from the beginning. If nothing else, thank Him because you are still breathing.

H: HAVE FAITH

"Faith comes by hearing, and hearing by the word of God" (Romans 10:17).

We have to work earnestly to increase our faith by meditating on the Word of God daily. We have to also activate our faith to see God in action. God does not require our faith to be as big as the mountains before He responds; He just wants us to trust in His supreme power. In Luke 17:6, Jesus said, "If you have faith as a mustard seed, you can say to this mulberry tree, 'Be pulled up by the roots and be planted in the sea,' and it would obey you." Jesus repeatedly commented on the power of faith in God, and why is it crucial that we act on our faith. In Matthew 17:20, He said, "For assuredly, I say to you, if you have faith as a mustard seed, you will say to this mountain, 'Move from here to there,' and it will move; and nothing will be impossible for you." He also made a similar remark in Matthew 21:21.

In the Bible, there are men and women of God who acted on their faith and it yielded unprecedented results, worthy of emulation in this day and age. We have to act on our faith, putting it to work, for faith without work is dead (James 2:17). We have to have a faith that endures, a faith that does not waver or doubt for a second God's ability to change a situation instantaneously. Peter showed this kind of faith in Matthew 14:28–31, when he stepped out of the boat and began to walk on the sea toward Jesus. As he realized he was actually walking on water, he began to sink, yet he called out to Jesus in faith, believing strongly that He would save him. We have to have the kind of faith the woman with the persistent hemorrhage had in Matthew 9:20–22, which made her say, "If only I may touch His garment, I shall be made well."

Furthermore, we have to have the kind of faith Queen Esther had in standing up for God's people (Esther 4–5). The kind of faith Elijah the prophet had when he declared drought in the land, when he encountered the widow at Zarephath, and when he commanded fire to consume his sacrifice during his challenge to the prophets of Baal (1 Kings 17–18). We have to have the kind of faith that Deborah the prophetess had when she portrayed not only her faith but also the courage, strength, and leadership of a faithful woman of God (Judges 4:12–5:31). Read more examples of faith in 2 Kings 4–5; 1 Samuel 1.

H: HUMBLE YOURSELF

"God resists the proud, but gives grace to the humble. Therefore humble yourselves under the mighty hand of God, that He may exalt you in due time" (1 Peter 5:5–6; James 4:6, 10).

Humility is what God requires of us, not to boast of our greatness but of His greatness, and to humble ourselves in service to His name (Micah 6:8; Luke 22:26).

I: INCREASE YOUR FAITH

> "But also for this very reason, giving all diligence, add to your faith virtue, to virtue knowledge, to knowledge self-control, to self-control perseverance, to perseverance godliness, to godliness brotherly kindness, and to brotherly kindness love. For if these things are yours and abound, you will be neither barren nor unfruitful in the knowledge of our Lord Jesus Christ. For he who lacks these things is shortsighted, even to blindness, and has forgotten that he was cleansed from his old sins. Therefore, brethren, be even more diligent to make your call and election sure, for if you do these things you will never stumble." (2 Peter 1:5–10)

You are also increasing in your faith when you apply the teachings of Jesus Christ and do those things He said would demonstrate the life of the righteous, things like feeding the hungry, clothing the naked, visiting and praying for the sick and those in prison. Jesus said that when we do these things, we are doing them for Him (Matthew 25:35–40).

J: JUDGE NOT, SO YOU WILL NOT BE JUDGED

"Judge not, that you be not judged. For with what judgment you judge, you will be judged; and with the measure you use, it will be measured back to you. And why do you look at the speck in your brother's eye, but do not consider the plank in your own eye? Or how can you say to your brother, 'Let me remove the speck from your eye'; and look, a plank is in your own eye? Hypocrite! First remove the plank from your own eye, and then you will see clearly to remove the speck from your brother's eye." (Matthew 7:1–5)

This word from Jesus is so powerful that I strongly believe it relates most certainly to everyone in one way or another. There are some people who think that they are perfect, spotless, and without fault. They spend most of their time finding fault in others, criticizing and judging their fellow human beings without examining themselves first. Jesus told us to always examine ourselves first to make sure we are not committing the same sin we are judging in others (Romans 2:1). We should not judge people based on their appearance, as Jesus pointed out in John 7:24, or judge without any knowledge or investigation into that person's history. Judgment belongs to God, the one who is able to save and destroy. He is our lawgiver; He is our judge and our king (Isaiah 33:22).

K: KINDNESS TO ONE ANOTHER

"Let all bitterness, wrath, anger, clamor, and evil speaking be put away from you, with all malice. And be kind to one another, tenderhearted, forgiving one another, even as God in Christ forgave you" (Ephesians 4:31–32).

In an ideal Christendom, there would be no anger, bitterness, ill speaking, jealousy, gossiping, or malice, but often you see all these behaviors and feelings. I see these as the work of the enemy; the devil wants to steal the peace and joy of the children of God. A person who envies somebody else's success or spends their time speaking ill and gossiping about others will have no peace of mind and no joy. Jesus told us in John 10:10, "The thief does not come except to steal, and to kill, and to destroy," but He came that we may have abundant life.

K: KNOW HIS LOVE

"That He would grant you, according to the riches of His glory, to be strengthened with might through His Spirit in the inner man, that Christ may dwell in your hearts through faith; that you, being rooted and grounded in love, may be able to comprehend with all the saints what is the width and length and depth and height—to know the love of Christ which passes knowledge; that you may be filled with all the fullness of God. Now to Him who is able to do exceedingly abundantly above all that we ask or think, according to the power that works in us." (Ephesians 3:16–20).

In knowing the love of Christ, you learn to fear God. The fear of God is the beginning of knowledge (Proverbs 1:7). The Lord gives wisdom and speaks knowledge and understanding (Proverbs 2:6).

L: LOVE YOUR GOD

"Love the Lord your God with all your heart, with all your soul, with all your mind, and with all your strength" (Mark 12:30).

God wants us to put Him first in everything. He wants us to serve Him and no other. He made this clear to us in several places in the Bible where He said, "I am the Lord and there is no other" (Isaiah 43:11; 44:6; 45:5–6, 14, 18).

L: LOVE YOUR NEIGHBORS

"You shall love your neighbor as yourself" (Mark 12:31, James 2:8, Romans 13:10).

Love, although four letters, is very powerful and requires more from us as Christians. It takes a lot to love. This is why it is the first and the greatest of all the Commandments. In 1 Corinthians 13, the Bible tells us that it will profit us nothing if we call ourselves true Christians but have not love because love suffers long and is kind; it does not envy; love does not parade itself, nor behave rudely, it does not seek its own, and is not provoked; love does not think any evil. It does not rejoice in iniquity, but rather, it rejoices in the truth. Love never fails; bears all things, believes all things, hopes all things, and endures all things (1 Corinthians 13:4–8).

To perfect this teaching about love for God and one another, God first loved us because He is love and He sent His only Son, Jesus Christ, to die for our sin (1 John 4:7–11; John 3:16). In John 15:13, Jesus said, "Greater love has no one than this, than to lay down one's life for his friends." So, if God loves us this much, we ought to love Him back. We ought to show Him how much we love all that He has done for us by living for Him and worshiping Him into eternity.

M: MAKE JESUS YOUR PERSONAL LORD AND SAVIOR.

When you make Jesus your personal Lord and Savior, your relationship with Him will be personal. You will serve Him because of the love you have for Him, not because of what you want to get from Him, but because of who He is to you. When you make God your personal Lord and Savior, you are not serving Him because Mr. A or Mrs. B is serving Him. You desire to serve Him from the bottom of your heart. You know you are living for Him; you hunger after the things of the Lord, and you serve Him in truth and in spirit.

When you make Jesus your personal Lord and Savior, He will be your way, your truth, and your life (John 14:6), and your only Savior (Acts 4:12). When you believe in Jesus and make Him your personal Lord and Savior, everlasting life will be your portion, as He promised in John 3:16.

M: MASTERPIECE

You are God's masterpiece, one of a kind and unique in your own ways! You are fearfully and wonderfully made in His image.

God has you in the palm of His hand. You are His masterpiece. "For by grace you have been saved through faith, and that not of yourselves; it is the gift of God, not of works, lest anyone should boast. For we are His workmanship, created in Christ Jesus for good works, which God prepared beforehand that we should walk in them" (Ephesians 2:8–10).

Therefore, as the workmanship of the Almighty, the masterpiece of God, you are carrying the image of God, so don't put on any image or allow anybody to put on you an image that does not represent God. Paul said, "By the mercies of God . . . present your bodies a living sacrifice, holy, acceptable to God, which is your reasonable service." As a masterpiece, you should esteem yourself as such, knowing that there is no other you. Do not compare yourself to another person or try to be like someone else. Have confidence in the Holy Spirit who lives in you and makes you who you are. Don't let the devil fool you or poison your heart and mind, turning you away from what you know about your God. Remember 1 Peter 5:8, which says the devil roams like a roaring lion, looking for whom to devour. You have to be alert both spiritually and physically. You have to also be prayerful, because prayer is a powerful weapon you will need to conquer the enemy.

N: Never Give Up

Never give up, even when it seems as if all hope is gone. Perhaps you feel you have given it your best shot. You may be closer than you think. Just give it another try and never give up trying.

Never give in, no matter the pressure. Stick to the fight, even when you are hit the hardest. It is when things seem at their worst during trials and tribulation that you must never give up. In the midst of all the tribulation, God is telling you to be still and know He is God. He is with you; He is your refuge (Psalm 46:10–11). Remember God's promise to us in 2 Corinthians 4:8–9, "We are hard-pressed on every side, yet not crushed; we are perplexed, but not in despair; persecuted, but not forsaken; struck down, but not destroyed." Remind yourself, even when you walk through the deepest valley, the Lord is with you (Psalm 23:4).

Never quit; quitters never win and winners never quit. Even when things go wrong, as they sometimes will, when the road seems so narrow and the going is getting tough, keep pressing harder, keep praying, and know that the fourth Man in the fiery furnace will be with you (Daniel 3:23–25).

Even when it seems as though there is no help from anywhere, there are no resources, and you are getting overwhelmed with heavy burdens, just know your help will come from the Lord, who made heaven and earth (Psalm 121:2). When you feel pressed down with so many things in this life, keep trying. With time, things will get better. Believe you can do all things though Christ who strengthens you (Philippians 4:13).

Never quit doing good. There is more blessing in doing good than in acting selfishly, more blessing in giving than in receiving. Even when others mistreat you, know your actions are for God, and God will surely reward you double for your trouble. Remember Galatians 6:9–10, which tells us not to grow weary while doing good, for in due season you shall reap if you do not lose heart. So, as we have opportunity, do good to all, especially to those who are of the household of faith.

O: OBEY HIS VOICE

In Jeremiah 7:23, God commands us, His children, to obey His voice, because He is our God, and we are His people. He said it will be well with us, if we walk in all the ways that He has commanded us. It is rewarding to be obedient to the voice of the Lord and to keep His commandments. God stipulates in Deuteronomy 28:1–14 the blessing that will follow those who obey His voice and His commandment. He says that the fruit of your body shall be blessed. You shall be blessed in the city and in the country; you shall be blessed in your going out and in your coming in. He will cause your enemies to be defeated. His blessings will follow you everywhere you go and in everything you touch. The Lord will open the heavenly blessings on you, rains to fall and water your lands and your crops and to bless your handiwork. He will allow you to lend to many and not borrow from anyone. He will make you the head and not the tail; you shall be above and not beneath. There is great blessing in obeying the voice of the Lord.

Even when we don't want to obey the voice of the Lord, even when we want to run away from doing what God has asked us to do, God has a way of pressing us to do what He wants us to do.

P: PRAY WITHOUT CEASING

"Praying always with all prayer and supplication in the Spirit, being watchful to this end with all perseverance and supplication for all the saints" (Ephesians 6:18).

Pray both in good times and in bad times. "Pray without ceasing" (1 Thessalonians 5:17). Pray even when you are overwhelmed with things of this life. Pray because that's how you will get through any situation you find yourself in. Pray and be patient with God (James 5:7–8).

Pray, for there is power in praying. Jesus said, "And whatever things you ask in prayer, believing, you will receive" (Matthew 21:22).

Pray, for that's how you will be filled with the Holy Spirit and power so that you will be able to stand against the worldly powers and spiritual forces. The Bible says in Ephesians 6:12–13, "We do not wrestle against flesh and blood, but against principalities, against powers, against the rulers of the darkness of this age, against spiritual hosts of wickedness in the heavenly places. Therefore [pray and] take up the whole armor of God, that you may be able to withstand in the evil day, and having done all, to stand."

Always PUSH (Pray Until Something Happens), and don't give up on your prayer. Keep praying until something happens, just like Elijah prayed for rain in 1 Kings 18:30–46. In the Bible, many other men and women of God prayed until something happened. Jabez prayed in 1 Chronicles 4:10 and something happened. God granted him all that he requested and changed his destiny for good.

Q: QUICK TO LISTEN

In James 1:19–20, the Word of God tells us to be quick to listen, slow to speak, and slow in anger, "for the wrath of man does not produce the righteousness of God." As Christians, we have to be quick to listen and think before we talk. When we ponder a thought before we talk, it helps us articulate our words better and prevents us from saying something stupid or something we will regret afterward. Also we have to be slow to anger. It is okay to get upset about something or get angry with somebody for whatever reason, but we should not let the anger put us into any distress. When we are slow to anger, it will help us maintain our peace of mind. The Bible tells us in Ephesians 4:26–27 not to let the sun go down on our anger or to give place to the devil.

R: RIGHT WITH GOD

"Therefore, having been justified by faith, we have peace with God through our Lord Jesus Christ, through whom also we have access by faith into this grace in which we stand, and rejoice in hope of the glory of God. And not only that, but we also glory in tribulations, knowing that tribulation produces perseverance; and perseverance, character; and character, hope. Now hope does not disappoint, because the love of God has been poured out in our hearts by the Holy Spirit who was given to us." (Romans 5:1–5)

When you are justified by faith, you have been put right with God, and if God through His infinite mercy and compassion does not condemn you, do not condemn yourself. Believe in the salvation Jesus came to give, for God did not send His Son, Jesus Christ, to condemn the world, rather He sent Him to redeem the world (John 3:17–18). Therefore, do not dwell on your past. Yesterday is gone; today is a gift from God, so make it right with Him today, so that you can walk with Him at all times in future—your tomorrow.

S: SEEK TO DO HIS WILL

Seek first God's kingdom and His righteousness, and every other thing shall be added to you (Matthew 6:33). When you seek to do God's will, you will see yourself growing spiritually. You will be filled with spiritual power, which you need to wear as an armor to enable you stand against the wiles of the devil. "For we do not wrestle against flesh and blood, but against principalities, against powers, against the rulers of the darkness of this age, against spiritual hosts of wickedness in the heavenly places" (Ephesians 6:12).

T: THANKSGIVING

The importance of thanksgiving can never be underestimated or overemphasized. There are numerous biblical principles on thanksgiving. Thanksgiving and prayer work hand-in-hand.

We show gratitude to God and thank Him for His goodness, grace, and mercy over our lives.

The Bible says in 1 Thessalonians 5:18, that what God requires of us is to give thanks in all circumstances. I believe this, because God is the Almighty. He knows the end from the beginning.

Ephesians 5:20 says to always give thanks and for everything "to God the Father in the name of our Lord Jesus Christ." Psalm 107:1 says, "Oh, give thanks to the Lord, for He is good! For His mercy endures forever."

Psalm 92:1–2 says that it is right to give thanks to the Lord and to sing praises for His lovingkindness in the morning and His faithfulness every night. Singing praises and worship to God in thanksgiving should always be an important aspect of our Christian life, because it allows us to appreciate God for all that He has done for us.

T: TRUST IN THE LORD

"Trust in the Lord with all your heart, and lean not on your own understanding; in all your ways acknowledge Him, and He shall direct your paths" (Proverbs 3:5–6). "Trust in the Lord and do good" (Psalm 37:3).

To trust in the Lord is to have faith, to have hope, and to be convinced of who God is. When you trust in the Lord, you are totally dependent on Him to lead your way, and you rely on Him with confidence knowing that He will not disappoint you. Do not put your trust in men, because they will fail you one day, but God never fails. God is the same yesterday, today, and forever (Hebrews 13:8), and His words are yes and amen (2 Corinthians 1:20).

U: USE THE GIFTS GOD HAS GIVEN YOU

As the children of God, we have been gifted in many ways. The Word of God in Romans 12:4–8 says,

> For as we have many members in one body, but all the members do not have the same function, so we, being many, are one body in Christ, and individually members of one another. Having then gifts differing according to the grace that is given to us, let us use them: if prophecy, let us prophesy in proportion to our faith; or ministry, let us use it in our ministering; he who teaches, in teaching; he who exhorts, in exhortation; he who gives, with liberality; he who leads, with diligence; he who shows mercy, with cheerfulness.

So, what are you good at? Take time to examine yourself and find out your calling in life. In other words, what is God's purpose in your life? It is a treasure you have to explore to discover. When you discover your gift, what you are really good at, go for it and use it for the glory of God. Do not get discouraged along the way, but trust God to lead you. James

1:17 tells us, "Every good gift and every perfect gift is from above, and comes down from the Father of lights, with whom there is no variation or shadow of turning."

V: VISION

What do you see?

What's your dream?

What are your expectations?

What's your visualization?

Do you see yourself becoming who God wants you to be?

Do you see yourself overcoming obstacles?

Do you see yourself lending and not borrowing?

Do you see yourself out of debt?

Do you see yourself succeeding?

Do you see yourself conquering?

Do you see yourself victorious?

Do you see yourself beating addiction?

Do you see yourself healed?

Do you see yourself overcoming your background?

Do you see yourself as a spellbreaker? Are you one who will stand and pray with authority, who will see things start happening, the chains of the enemy broken, and generational curses destroyed? Are you one who will pray and deliver your family from bondage? Will you pray for a breakthrough to your life and the lives of those around you? Do you see yourself as the light of God shining in darkness?

Do you see yourself with peace of mind?

Do you see your God working out your miracle? He has never failed and will never fail. He does everything He says He will do. Do you see Him working in your favor? Do you see Him fighting your battle? Do you see Him bringing you your miracle?

Do you see yourself _____? Please fill in the blank with whatever you see yourself becoming, because there is power in your words. Proverbs 18:21 says, "Death and life are in the power of the tongue." So speak life over your life and over your situation.

In Ezekiel 37:1–14, God challenged Ezekiel with the power of prophecy and the power of right believing, to prophesy to the dry bones and to believe they will live again. He did as he was commanded and the dry bones came back to life again. In Genesis 15:5, God told Abram (Abraham), "Look now toward heaven, and count the stars if you are able to number them. So shall your descendants be."

Declare and believe without doubt and heaven will be in agreement with you. The Word of God says in Matthew 18:18, "Whatever you bind on earth will be bound in heaven, and whatever you loose on earth will be loosed in heaven." And in Job 22:28, the Word of God says you should declare a word and it shall be established for you. So declare what you want to see happening in your life, and it shall come to pass!

W: WORSHIP

"Give to the Lord the glory due His name; bring an offering, and come before Him. Oh, worship the Lord in the beauty of holiness!" (1 Chronicles 16:29).

"But the hour is coming, and now is, when the true worshipers will worship the Father in spirit and truth; for the Father is seeking such to worship Him. God is Spirit, and those who worship Him must worship in spirit and truth" (John 4:23–24).

Worship God every moment of your life, regardless of the situation. Through worship, you connect with heaven and enter God's presence and glory. When you connect with heaven during praising and worshiping, heavenly choirs and saints sing and worship with you, because that's all they do twenty-four/seven before the throne of the Almighty God.

Prayer and worship go hand-in-hand. When you are going through certain circumstances, sometimes all you have to do is worship and leave the battle to God. He will fight your battle for you; you will see God moving in an amazing way. The Israelites sang and worshiped in Joshua 6, and the wall of Jericho fell.

W: WALK IN THE LIGHT OF GOD

"But if we walk in the light as He is in the light, we have fellowship with one another, and the blood of Jesus Christ His Son cleanses us from all sin." (1 John 1:7).

"O house of Jacob, come and let us walk in the light of the Lord" (Isaiah 2:5).

Walk in the light of God, for God is light. This is a metaphor, a figure of speech that is deep and diverse in meaning. To walk in the light is to live in righteousness, to seek after God who Himself is light, to do away with evil and run from darkness, to always do the right thing at all times and to desire to live for Christ. In John 8:12, Jesus said, "I am the light of the world. He who follows Me shall not walk in darkness, but have the light of life." Ephesians 5:8 tells us to walk as children of light, for we are now light in the Lord.

W: WAIT ON THE LORD

"Wait on the Lord; be of good courage, and He shall strengthen your heart; wait I say, on the Lord" (Psalm 27:14).

To wait on the Lord is to relax your mind and not worry or be consumed with worry. It is to patiently and expectantly trust and believe God will show up and answer your prayers. Even if it seems as though He's taking a long time, keep waiting on Him. In due time, He will surely show Himself mighty in your life. Know that God's delay is never a denial. Lamentations 3:25 says the Lord is good to those who wait on Him. "Those who wait on the Lord," Isaiah tells us, "shall renew their strength; they shall mount up with wings like eagles, they shall run and not be weary, and they shall walk and not faint" (Isaiah 40:31).

X: EXTRAORDINARY

You are an eXtraordinary child of the Most High God. God is the God that makes the ordinary eXtraordinary. Our God is not an ordinary God, therefore you, His child, you are not ordinary. You are an eXtraordinary child of God, created in the image of God. God says in Jeremiah 1:5 that even before you were formed in the womb, He knew you; even before you were born, He sanctified you, and He ordained you as a prophet to the nations. So you have to take off any clothes of defeat or low self-esteem. You have to change your mindset and shake off any spirit of sadness, oppression, and suppression. Know that your heavenly Father is the king of the whole universe, and you are His son or daughter, prince or princess.

God has a way of using the ordinary in eXtraordinary ways. God's purpose for you is to see you reach your highest potential. His plan for you is of good and not of evil; to give you a future and a hope, as He promised in Jeremiah 29:11. God has more for you; therefore do not relent in your love and desire for His blessings. Of His eXtraordinary plans for you, the Bible says in 1 Corinthians 2:9, that no mind has imagined, and eyes have not seen it, nor have ears heard what God has prepared for those who love Him.

Y: YOU HAVE THE POWER

The power and the authority have already been given to you. Exercise them. It only takes you believing in God. Jesus said, "And these signs will follow those who believe: In My name they will cast out demons; they will speak with new tongues; they will take up serpents; and if they drink anything deadly, it will by no means hurt them; they will lay hands on the sick, and they will recover" (Mark 16:17–18). In Luke 10:19, God says, "I give you the authority to trample on serpents and scorpions, and over all the power of the enemy, and nothing shall by any means hurt you." In Matthew 16:19, He says that He "will give you the keys of the kingdom of heaven, and whatever you bind on earth will be bound in heaven, and whatever you loose on earth will be loosed in heaven."

So use these powers God has put in you to unlock your gifts and your potential: the power of right believing, the power of positive thinking, and the power of prayer. When you pray, pray with authority; it has already been given to you from heaven. So use it to enter the domain of the enemy to get back everything belonging to you that the enemy has stolen from you, whether it is your health, your peace, your joy, your finances, your success, your progress, your opportunities, your promotions, your family, or your children. You have to recover all. Believe and declare it, and it shall come to pass.

Z: ZEALOUS FOR GOD

Are you zealous for the Lord God of Hosts?

Do you go after Him?

Do you put Him first in your life?

God wants us to put Him first, to serve Him and no other god. As children of God, we have to be zealous about our faith in God, just like the prophet Elijah was very zealous for the Lord God of Hosts in 1 Kings 19:10, and as Jehu was in 2 Kings 10:16. God wants us to be passionate for Him and to love Him with all our hearts, as in Deuteronomy 6:5. He wants to see enthusiastic followers. He wants to see us zealously going after

Him. God said in Jeremiah 29:13, "You will seek Me and find Me, when you search for Me with all your heart." We have to show our enthusiasm just like the apostles did in Act 2:42, when they preached the good news of God. We have to be zealous also in our prayers, for the Bible says the "effective, fervent, [zealous], prayer of the righteous man avails much" (James 5:16).

Printed in the United States
By Bookmasters